D0538708

/

DRAWING WITH YOUR
Fingerprints

GODELEINE DE ROSAMEL

Gareth Stevens Publishing
A WORLD ALMANAC EDUCATION GROUP COMPANY

Please visit our web site at: www.garethstevens.com
For a free color catalog describing Gareth Stevens Publishing's list
of high-quality books and multimedia programs, call 1-800-542-2595 (USA) or
1-800-387-3178 (Canada). Gareth Stevens Publishing's fax: (414) 332-3567.

Library of Congress Cataloging-in-Publication Data

De Rosamel, Godeleine.
    [Dessine avec tes empreintes. English]
    Drawing with your fingerprints/by Godeleine De Rosamel.
        p. cm. — (Drawing is easy)
    Summary: Step-by-step illustrations demonstrate how to use fingerprints
as the starting point for drawings.
    Includes bibliographical references.
    ISBN 0-8368-3628-6 (lib. bdg.)
    1. Drawing—Technique—Juvenile literature.   2. Fingerprints in art—Juvenile
literature. [1. Drawing—Technique.   2. Fingerprints in art.]   I. Title.
NC655.R66913   2003
741.2—dc21   2002036539

This edition first published in 2003 by
Gareth Stevens Publishing
A World Almanac Education Group Company
330 West Olive Street, Suite 100
Milwaukee, WI 53212 USA

This edition © 2003 by Gareth Stevens, Inc.
First published as *Dessine: Avec tes empreintes* in 2000 by Editions Casterman.
© 2000 by Casterman. Additional end matter © 2003 by Gareth Stevens, Inc.

Translation: Patrice Lantier
Gareth Stevens editor: Dorothy L. Gibbs
Gareth Stevens designer: Melissa Valuch
Cover design: Melissa Valuch

Printed in the United States of America

1 2 3 4 5 6 7 8 9 07 06 05 04 03

Table of Contents

1

2

thumbprint

3

4

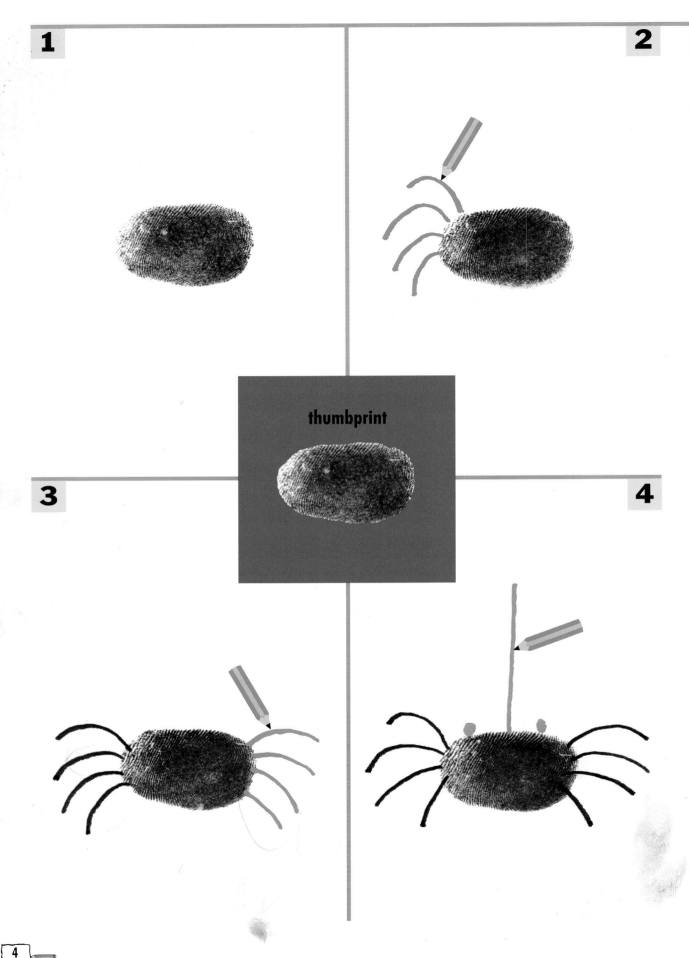

a spider

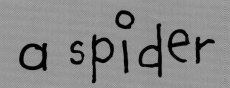

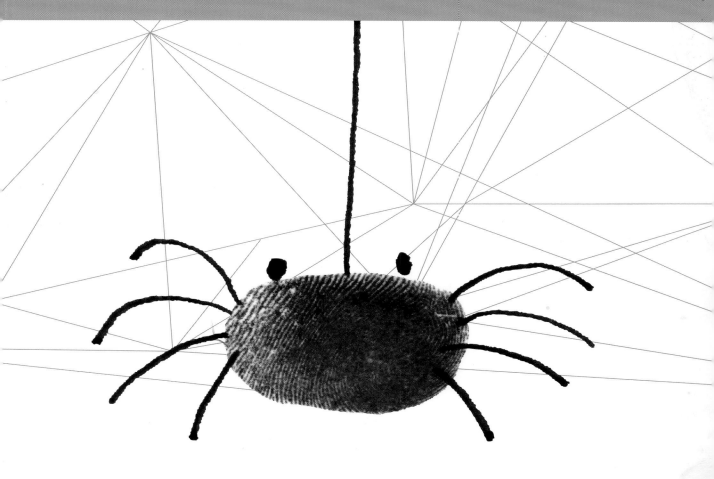

a mosquito   **a bee**   **a fly**   **a snail**

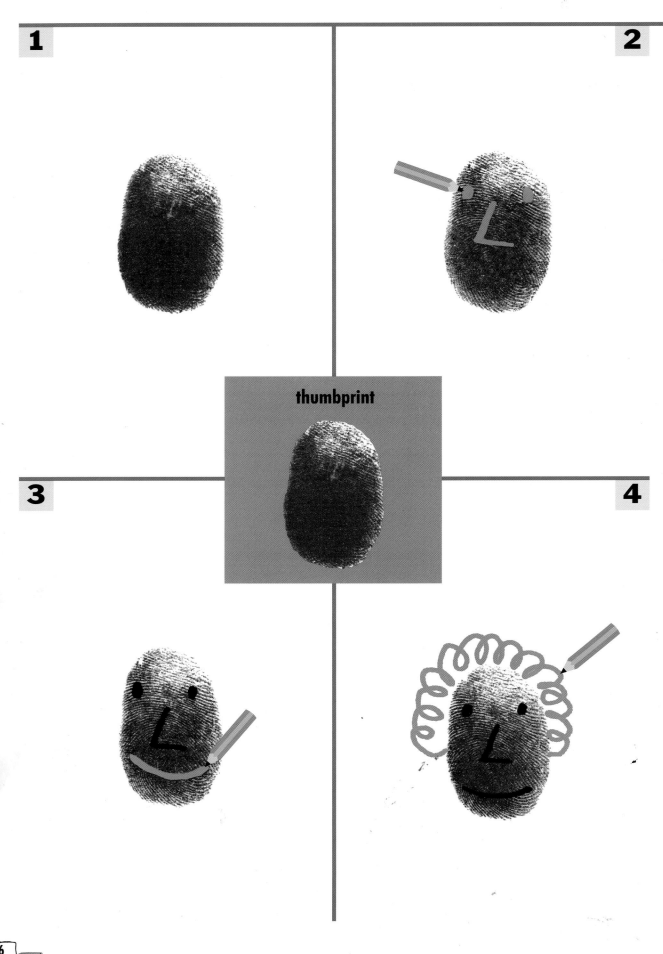

1

2

thumbprint

3

4

6

a face

a boy's face   **a man's face**   **a girl's face**   **a baby's face**

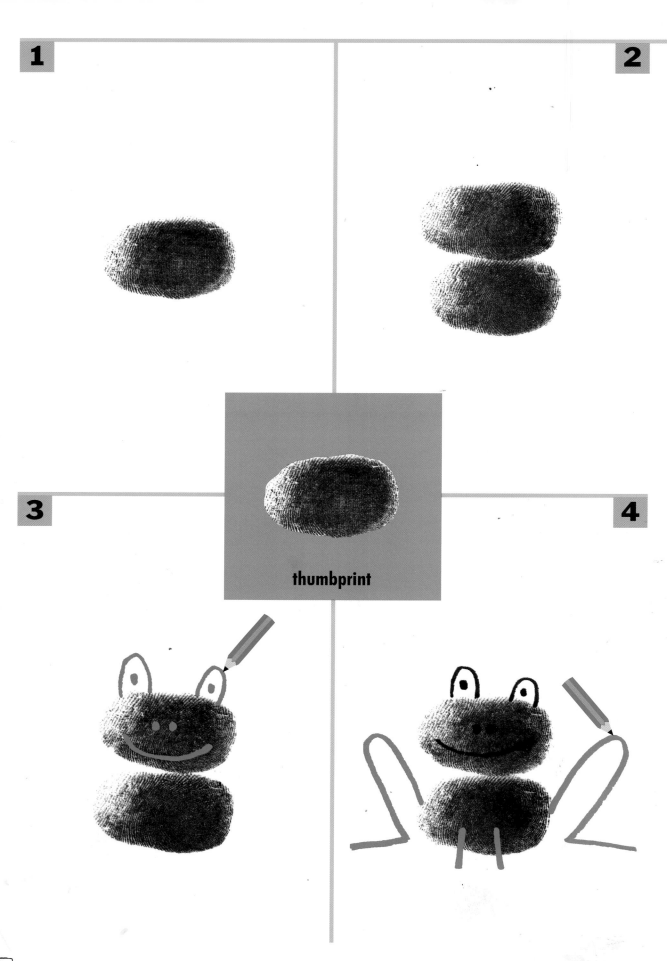

1

2

thumbprint

3

4

8

a frog

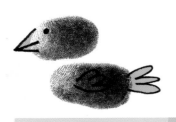

a bird   **a pig**   **a cat**   **an owl**

1

thumbprint

2

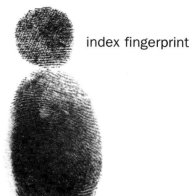

index fingerprint

index fingerprint

thumbprint

3

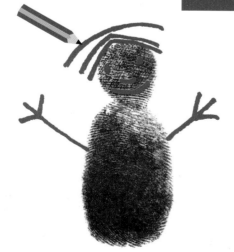

4

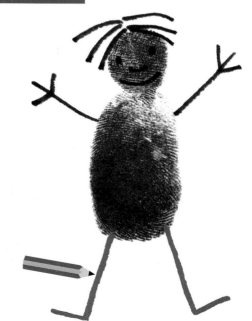

a juggler

index fingerprint

thumbprint

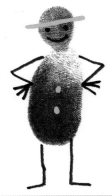

| a baby | a person running | a person jumping | a man |

1

2

thumbprints

index fingerprint

thumbprint

3

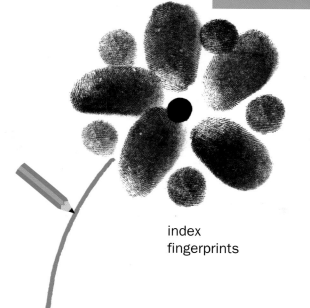

index
fingerprints

4

thumbprints

two flowers

a poppy   **a leaf**   **a fern**   **a daisy**

1

2

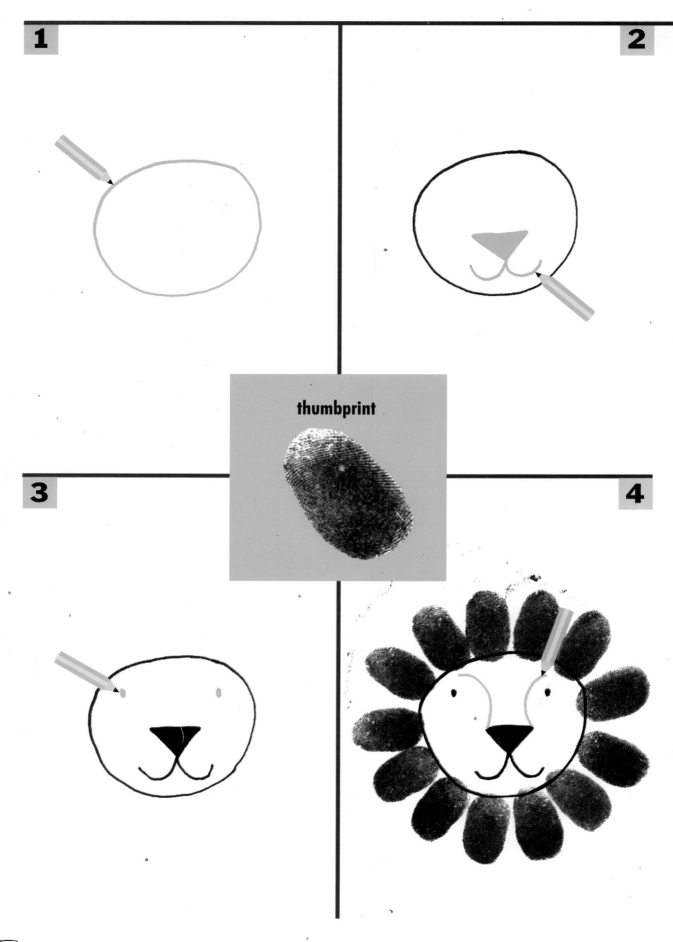

thumbprint

3

4

a LioN

thumbprints

a rooster

index
fingerprints

a chicken

a lion cub

a koala

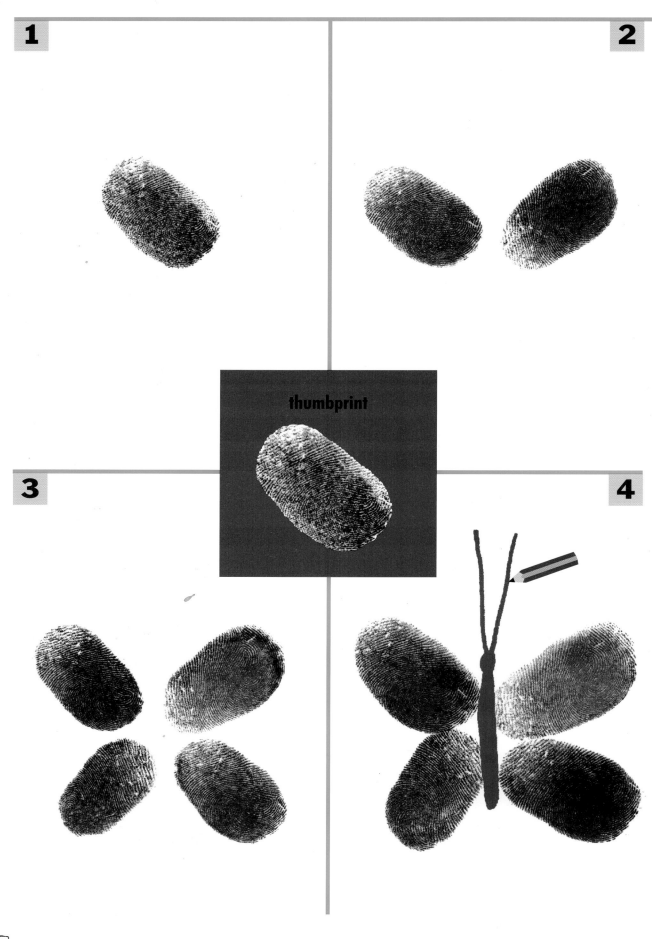

1

2

thumbprint

3

4

a butterfly

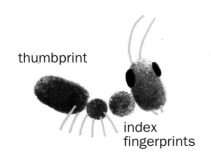

thumbprint

index
fingerprints

| an ant | a dragonfly | a caterpillar |

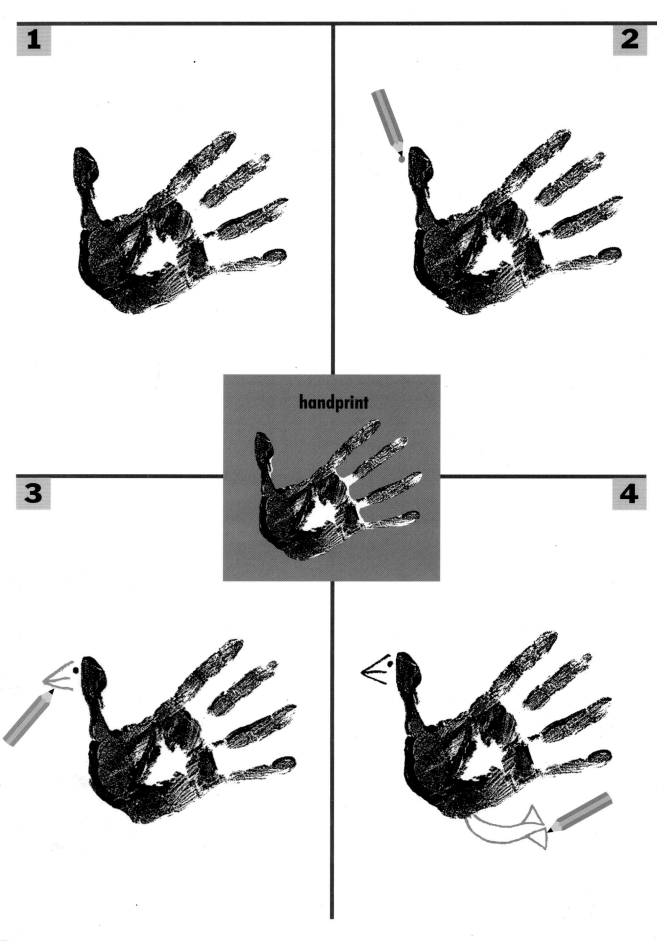

1

2

handprint

3

4

18

a duck

| an octopus | a rooster | a giraffe |

1

left hand

2

right hand

handprint

3

4

a bat

a moose | a bird flying

right fist

left fist

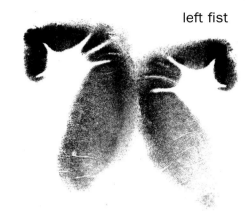

fist print

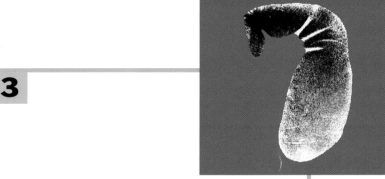

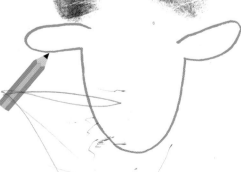
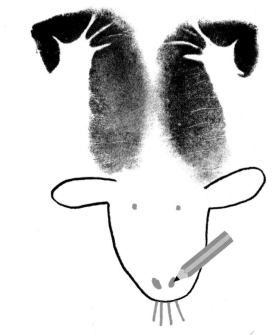

a ram

a water buffalo   **a scorpion**   **an antelope**   **a crab**

more drawing books

- *Draw Thumb Things: Fine Art at Your Fingertips*
  (Klutz Press)

- *Ed Emberley's Fingerprint Drawing Book*
  Ed Emberley
  (Little, Brown and Company)

- *Hand-Print Animal Art*
  Carolyn Carreiro
  (Econo-Clad Books)

web sites

- Fingerprint Characters
  www.dltk-kids.com/crafts/miscellaneous/fingerprint_characters.htm

- Thumbthing Creative
  www.geocities.com/sousonne/Tprints.html